The princess and the frog

Once upon a time, in a far off land, lived a kind old king and queen. They lived in a huge empty palace with their only daughter, the princess.

The kind old king and queen were sad because their only daughter, who they loved so much, was sad.

The princess was sad because she didn't have any brothers or sisters. She hated living all by herself in the huge empty palace.

"If I never meet any princes," she cried to herself as she sat under the old oak tree, "I will never marry. If I never marry I will live all by myself for the rest of my life in this huge empty palace."

"Please don't cry,"
said the kind old king.

"I hate to see you so sad. Why are you so sad, my little princess?"

"I am sad because I don't have any brothers or sisters, and if I don't meet any princes I will never marry. If I never marry I will live all by myself for the rest of my life in this huge empty palace."

"Don't cry," said the kind old queen. "It will soon be your birthday and we will have a party. We will have the biggest and best party any princess has ever had. We will invite all the princes in the kingdom, and lots of other people too."

To make their sad little princess happy the kind old king and queen gave her a very special present.

It was a ball, but a very special ball.
It was not a rubber ball.
It was not a plastic ball.
It was a gold ball, a solid gold ball!
"Thank you," she smiled.
"I will keep this golden ball for ever."

As the princess played all by herself with her golden ball, the servants made the palace ready for the party.

They hung flags and ribbons and hundreds of balloons – red balloons, green balloons, yellow and blue balloons – all over the palace.

9

Princes and princesses came from all over the kingdom, and lots of other people came too.

The band played, the clowns did tricks and the chimps ran off with the crown!

There was a feast of jelly, and huge piles of cakes and other good things to eat.

But the princess still felt sad.
"Why are all the princes in the kingdom so silly?" she asked her mother.

Then, sobbing, she ran down the steps and into the garden, and slumped down under the old oak tree.

But she tripped and fell, and her golden ball fell from her pocket and rolled down the hill.
Splash! Into the water it fell and sank to the bottom of the lake.
"Oh, no! Now I shall never see my golden ball again," cried the princess.

It was turning into a *very* bad day for the little princess!

Now, all this time, the little green frog, who always sat on the little green lily pad, had been watching the princess.

"Croak! Croak!" went the little green frog, as he dived into the lake. Down and down into the cold water he swam until he found the golden ball. Then up and up he struggled.

The princess was so happy, she gave the little green frog a big kiss.

"Oh, my princess!" said the handsome prince. "Your kiss has broken the wicked witch's spell. Thank you. Thank you!"

The kind old king and queen were so pleased to see the princess so happy that they told the frog prince that he could live with them in the palace as long as he wished.

The prince and princess grew to love each other so much that one day the prince asked the princess to marry him.

Soon, the two were married, and they both lived happily ever after.

16